PET OWNER'S GUIDE TO THE
BULL TERRIER

Peter Larkin

RINGPRESS

ABOUT THE AUTHOR

Peter Larkin, a retired veterinary surgeon, acquired his first Bull Terrier which was a rescue dog, back in 1952. But it was in 1960 that he became interested in starting his own breeding programme, and he and his wife bought their first bitch from the famous Romany kennel. This was the start of the Booksale line which has enjoyed considerable success in the show ring.

Peter has served on the committee of the Bull Terrier Club for many years, acting as chairman before his retirement. He is a specialist judge of Bull Terriers, and has travelled worldwide on judging appointments. Both his wife and his daughter judge the breed in the UK and overseas.

A member of the Kennel Club, Peter has served on its scientific committee, with special reference to the interbreeding of standard and miniature Bull Terriers.

Photography: Sheila Atter.

Cover: Ch. Arcanum Kalamkari ('Smiler'),
bred and owned by Andrea and Brian Hill.

Published by Ringpress Books,
Vincent Lane, Dorking, Surrey,
RH4 3YX, England.

First published 2000
© Interpet Publishing. All rights reserved

ISBN 1 86054 100 3

Printed and bound in Hong Kong through Printworks International Ltd.

CONTENTS

1 Introducing The Bull Terrier

The Bull Terrier – 'The Gladiator of the Canine Race' – was first developed by the dog-fighting community in the early 1800s from a cross between the Bulldog and the English Terrier. This sporting breed, which inherited its courage from the Bulldog, and its agility and tenacity from the Terrier, was primarily used for dog-fighting, ratting and bull and bear-baiting, and became known as the 'Bull-and-Terrier'.

The first Bull-and-Terriers were, by all accounts, rather comical, heavy and ugly dogs, inheriting much of their appearance – short, thick heads, blunt muzzles, undershot jaws, bow-legs and thick-set bodies – as well as their determination, from the Bulldog. Although these dogs were certainly odd-looking animals, those that had only a quarter to a half of Bulldog in their ancestry, and consequently were less undershot, gamely served the purpose for which they had been bred.

INFLUENTIAL BREEDERS

Unlike many breeds, where a large number of prominent breeders have influenced the general look and shape of the dogs, the Bull Terrier has only really had two people mould the breed to their ideal – James Hinks and Raymond Oppenheimer.

In 1835, a Bill of Parliament was passed, forbidding the cruel sports of bull and bear-baiting and also that of dog-fighting. After the passing of this Bill, although dog-fighting carried on in secret, many fanciers of the Bull-and-Terrier, being (perhaps surprisingly) fond of their dogs, abandoned their sport and became law-abiding citizens. They decided to concentrate on producing a better-looking dog, which still retained the courage, tenacity and

The coloured Bull Terrier was established after crossing with the Staffordshire Bull Terrier. This is Arcanum Capsicum.

faithfulness to humans for which their animals had become famous. It soon became apparent to those breeders who wanted a more aesthetically pleasing dog that further 'infusions' of terrier blood were needed.

With this in mind, in the early 1850s, James Hinks – known as the Father of the Bull Terrier – decided to further develop the breed by experimenting and crossing the Bull-and-Terrier with the White English Terrier and possibly the Dalmatian. The result was a strain of all-white dogs, which he called 'Bull Terriers'.

These new dogs, two of the most famous being Old Puss and Quick, were longer and cleaner of head, stronger in foreface and free from lippiness – that is, they had tight-fitting muzzles. They also had longer, more elegant necks and cleaner body lines. They were generally more active and certainly more pleasing to look at. The Bull Terrier had become an alert, active, muscular and handsome dog that every 'man about town' wished to own.

In 1895, with the painful process of ear-cropping for Bull Terriers being banned, every effort was made by breeders to produce animals with neat upright ears, the first of these being a dog called Bloomsbury Charlewood.

The Bull Terrier then remained little changed, other than minor conformation improvements, right up to the time that the late Raymond Oppenheimer CBE, owner of the famous Ormandy prefix, started to take an interest in the breed. It is probably safe to say that Mr Oppenheimer is almost wholly responsible for giving the Bull Terrier his distinctive egg-shaped head and proud Roman nose.

THE BULL TERRIER CLUB

During the 1850s, the Bull Terrier also became a show dog, first appearing in the schedule of a show held in Leeds during the summer of 1852. Although the first dog shows were originally only for sporting breeds, they were soon extended and attracted the owners of ex-fighting dogs, who were thrilled to have the chance once more to compete, albeit only in beauty contests. As you can imagine, competition was fierce – as it is today – and breeders began to vie with one another to produce better and better-looking animals.

The Bull Terrier Club itself was formed by enthusiasts in 1887 and today has a worldwide membership of about 2,000. It is probably one of the oldest breed clubs in the United Kingdom – the Kennel Club itself only being formed in 1875 – and has associations with many other Bull Terrier clubs, both here in the United Kingdom and abroad.

COLOURED BULL TERRIERS

Although James Hinks's Bull Terriers were all-white, the original Bull-and-Terriers showed a variety of colours inherited from the Bulldog. Further crossing with Staffordshire Bull Terriers established the coloured Bull Terrier at the beginning of this century, although, due to a great deal of opposition, particularly to the colour-bred whites (whites bred from coloured parents), it was only in 1933 that they were officially recognised by the Kennel Club.

WORLD DOMINATION

Although the Bull Terrier is a British breed, it has gained worldwide popularity. As well as the parent club – the Bull Terrier Club – there are a dozen or so regional clubs in the United Kingdom. There are also clubs for Bull Terrier owners in the United States, South Africa, New Zealand, Australia and all over Europe, notably the Netherlands, Germany, Scandinavia and Belgium.

2 *Choosing A Bull Terrier*

Obviously, you and your family have thought long and hard about the type of dog you want. The fact that you have actually gone to the trouble of buying this book means that you are going about the business of obtaining the dog of your dreams in a sensible and responsible manner. However, is the Bull Terrier really the dog for you? Before plunging headlong into buying a puppy, you must be completely sure in your mind, and be able to assure the puppy's breeder, that this breed really is the one for you.

CHARACTERISTICS

The Bull Terrier, with his powerful physique and distinctive, egg-shaped head, could not really be mistaken for any other breed.

To many people who do not know the breed, the Bull Terrier – with his Roman nose and small eyes – is just plain ugly. In fact, on more than one occasion, a top winning champion has been compared to a goat or a pig on a lead! However, to those who love them, they are 'beautifully ugly', and have a charm all of their own. A charm, I might add, that is

The Bull Terrier is famous for its love of people.

appreciated not only by the ordinary person in the street, but also by Royalty.

Although the Kennel Club Standard – the breed's 'blueprint' if you like – does not specify any weight or height limits for the Bull Terrier, in general the dogs weigh approximately 60-70 lbs, and the bitches usually a little less perhaps below 50 lbs. There is a lot of dog packed into a relatively small frame, and, when they want to walk through the plate-glass door that is between them and the next-door neighbour's cat, there is not much that will stop them.

TEMPERAMENT

A Bull Terrier should not only be a bold and fearless fellow, but also display a loyal and good-natured personality. These requirements do not make him a Jekyll and Hyde character, but rather a self-confident, good-natured 'family dog', who is also something of a clown and enjoys playing to the gallery and entertaining his owner.

The breed is famous for its love of people, both young and old, and should approach strangers with confidence, showing no signs of fear or aggression. However, some Bull Terriers do not take too kindly to other dogs invading

their space. Although they never actually pick an argument, they know how to handle themselves in difficult situations and it is up to you, the owner, to be aware of this. Remember the Bull Terrier's fighting origins, and do not allow your Bull Terrier to get into those situations where he is likely to be threatened.

Although responsive to discipline, some Bull Terriers have been known to show an obstinate streak, and I promise that, unless you are prepared to provide firm, logical and affectionate training, you will give up before they do!

By nature the couch potato of the canine race, the Bull Terrier still demands a regular exercise routine.

EXERCISE NEEDS

If a Bull Terrier had his way, he would spend most of his days making a very passable imitation of a couch potato, moving from the best chair in the sitting room to a warm, sunny spot in the garden, and back again, preferably without using his legs. However, once roused, a Bull Terrier really does seem to enjoy nothing more than romping in the garden or field with his family and playing fetch – although, as the owner, you will be doing most of the fetching!

Seriously, and despite the fact that the Bull Terrier seems to adapt happily to living in the modern residential environment, in order for him to keep his athletic and muscular physique, you must not allow him to become a total couch potato. Both you and your dog will benefit considerably from steady and regular (i.e. daily) road-work and free playing, come rain or shine. Although a large garden is not essential, some secure, well-fenced space is required so that your Bull Terrier can stretch his legs and do his 'hot laps', when the need arises.

'Hot laps' seem to be a Bull Terrier phenomenon. The dog

In order to keep the Bull Terrier's athletic physique, he must be given regular exercise.

tucks his tail in, flattens his ears against his head and runs hell for leather over, through (never around) and under every object that gets in his way. This exercise only lasts a few minutes, but could well be the source of the saying: 'like a Bull (Terrier) in a china shop'!

PUPPY OR ADULT

When people think of acquiring a new dog, they automatically think of buying a puppy. They invariably have a mental picture of the cute little pup which will grow with them, and develop the kind of personality they want. However, lurking in the background of that wonderful picture is the sheer hard work involved in rearing and house-training a young animal.

For some people, particularly those who are not in the first flush of youth, it may be a better solution to give a home to an older dog. There are always Bull Terriers in welfare centres who, through no fault of their own, are looking for kind, loving and understanding new owners.

There are also some breeders who prefer to place dogs who have finished their show or breeding careers into loving pet homes. They believe that it is better for a dog who has worked hard for them, be it producing Champion progeny or winning many prizes, to finish his or her days in the lap of luxury – or the best chair anyway – as a pampered pet, rather than sit them out in a kennel, where they are just one of a number. Such dogs need not be old stagers, but could be as young as three or four years old.

So, unless your heart is absolutely set on buying that puppy, why not consider one of the above options?

Most people prefer to start with a puppy, but remember the hard work involved before taking one on.

DOG OR BITCH
Having made up your mind that the Bull Terrier really is the breed for you, then another decision to be made will be whether to have a dog or a bitch.

In some cases, this decision may have already been made for you, depending on the breeder and what puppy bookings they already have, and, obviously, what puppies the bitch produces. However, if you have never owned a Bull Terrier before, many owners and breeders will advise you to have a bitch, as they tend to be less dominant and more affectionate to their human family than the males, with their more 'macho' outlook on life. There are, however, other pros and cons to consider.

Male dogs, obviously, do not come into season, but their hormones are nonetheless active, and a determined male with fun and games (sex!) on his mind can prove to be something of an embarrassment if he is determined to wander, especially if the object of his desires is the Chair of the local Women's Institute, or, more seriously, a small child, to whom an over-zealous male could cause injury. Neutering the dog is a solution, but, as with neutered females, a castrated male tends to gain weight, and he may possibly undergo a slight personality change. Also, although you can get permission from the Kennel Club to show a neutered dog, the Standard does actually require the dog to have "two apparently normal testicles fully descended into the scrotum".

Bitches generally come into season twice a year, with the attendant oestrous discharge and the unwanted attention of any entire male dog in the neighbourhood. To avoid the inconvenience and mess caused by a bitch coming into season, treatments such as contraceptive

A bitch will probably be less dominant than a dog.

pills or injections are available from your veterinary surgeon to stop the seasons. A bitch can also be spayed, but, as with the neutered male, there is a tendency for a sterilised bitch to gain weight unless her diet is strictly regulated.

Do not think that, if you buy a bitch, you will be able to 'make money out of her' by having puppies. This is a misguided idea, and breeding dogs is only for the dedicated, knowledgeable and

A red and white Bull Terrier. The colour becomes brighter as the dog matures.

responsible. More importantly, if you breed and rear puppies properly, there is no money whatsoever to be made, and I can assure you that every reputable breeder will tell you that this is the case.

WHITE OR COLOURED

Every Bull Terrier owner and breeder, right from the very beginning, has a favourite colour. Some owners and breeders only have whites, some only have coloureds, and this is just one more decision that you are going to have to make. Do you prefer the clean lines of the all-white dog, possibly interrupted with a head or ear mark, or do you hanker after a smart tiger brindle with a white collar and feet?

The Bull Terrier Standard allows a variety of colours – white, brindle, red, fawn and tricolour – but blue and liver are highly undesirable, as these dogs tend to thrive less well, and also carry undesirable recessive genes. In a coloured Bull Terrier, the main colour, whichever it may be, predominates.

SEEKING ADVICE

All things being equal, you and your Bull Terrier are going to share many years of life together and the dog will become an important member of your family. So it makes a great deal of sense for you to spend some time making sure that you get the best possible puppy, and that you do everything that is humanly possible to avoid any problems.

In order to be able to form sensible opinions, and to help you and your family make all the right decisions, it is a good idea to seek advice from those in the know – owners and breeders of Bull Terriers themselves. The best place to track these strange creatures down is probably at one of the many dog shows held each year. Alternatively, contact your national kennel club for details of Bull Terrier clubs and speak to the club secretary. Explain that you are looking for a Bull Terrier puppy and that you are also interested in joining the club. On

joining, you will be notified of shows and special events being held by the club and, ideally, you should attend a few of these so that you have a chance to meet and talk to some of the breeders.

At these shows and events, seek out and talk to as many owners and breeders as you can, concentrating on those who are exhibiting the type of Bull Terrier you admire. You will find that these people are more than happy to talk to prospective owners, as long as it is not just before they are going into the ring to show their latest high-flyer. These kind souls will even point out the drawbacks as well as the virtues of owning a Bull Terrier. In the long run, it pays them to be frank, as no responsible breeder wants to place a puppy in a home where his life will be miserable.

CHOOSING THE RIGHT BREEDER

Do not rush into buying the first puppy you are offered, and in particular be wary of the breeder who immediately tells you they have just the puppy for you without even enquiring into your circumstances. Far better is the breeder who suggests you contact him or her a few days after the

It is important to decide whether you plan to complete in the show ring with your puppy. This is a promising 12-month-old youngster – Redinara Dennis The Menace

show or event to make an appointment to see the dogs at home. Before you even get invited to visit their kennels, you will have been asked all sorts of questions. You may feel that this questioning is an invasion of your privacy; however, if you are keen to own a Bull Terrier, you must appreciate that the breeder has to be sure that you will provide his or her precious puppy with a loving and secure home. Be honest and fair with breeders, and they in turn will be honest and fair with you.

PET OR SHOW

As well as answering all the lifestyle questions that the breeder will ask you, you no doubt will be asked whether you are interested in showing. If you are, do not pretend that you are only looking for a pet puppy, in the hope that the price will be lower. Likewise, if you are looking for a fireside companion, say so, and remember that you did not buy a show dog when, twelve months later, the local dog know-all tells you that you have a prospective Champion on the end of your lead.

There is nothing more annoying for a breeder than to sell to a pet home a perfectly healthy, typical puppy, who is not a top-quality show animal because of some minor show fault, only to find that the owner has been persuaded to show him. When the dog does not win and the judges point out his faults, the owner then gets cross with the breeder for selling them a 'pup', conveniently forgetting that the

You should be able to see the mother with her puppies.

puppy was not sold as a show prospect in the first place.

VISITING THE BREEDER

Once you have been interrogated over the telephone by the breeder of your choice, you will be invited to visit his or her kennels and see the adult dogs. Keep the appointment and arrive on time – breeders are busy people, and setting aside an hour or two of their time to entertain prospective owners means that vital chores have to be delayed. During your visit, ask any questions about the breed you feel have not yet been answered in your prior investigations. Do not worry about asking what you may feel are silly questions. It is far better to have the question answered,

and have a laugh and a joke about it, than to make a serious mistake that could have been avoided. Remember, we are all human, and your chosen breeder was once a novice Bull Terrier owner too.

Find out from the breeder when he or she expects to have a puppy available, and be prepared to wait to get the dog you really want. Most reputable breeders have waiting lists of prospective owners, and no Bull Terrier bitch, no matter how intelligent she is, can produce the right number of dog and bitch puppies to order. You may find that you have to wait months, but do not lose patience and buy the first puppy you see advertised, regardless of his breeding and origins. You may live to rue the day.

If the breeder tells you that a puppy may be available from a certain litter, ask to see the mother, and, if at all possible, the father as well. This may not always be possible, as most breeders travel to use the best available stud dogs.

Once you have decided that you are keen to purchase a puppy from your chosen breeder, discuss your preference with regard to sex and colour (if there is a likelihood of there being coloured puppies in the litter). If a puppy is likely to be available soon, the breeder may ask you for a deposit. This is not only a gesture of goodwill on your part, but also serves to weed out the time-wasters.

In due course, you will get that long-awaited call. It is, of course, possible that the bitch has not read the puppy order, and that the puppy available it is not the sex or colour you wanted. The breeder will, naturally, ask you to come and see the puppies anyway. However, think long and hard before committing even to just one visit. Are you prepared to have a dog instead of a bitch or a brindle instead of a white? If you want to stick to your original choice, then tell the breeder that you would prefer to wait and see

It helps if you can see the puppies in an outdoor environment.

A puppy with show potential must meet certain credentials. This red and white pup has perfect markings.

ASSESSING THE PUPPIES

Once the litter is born, arrange to visit them as often as is convenient to both you and the breeder.

Rather than being shown just 'your' puppy, ask politely to see the whole litter together. This way, it is possible to get an idea of how your puppy interacts with his or her siblings, and also for you to compare them physically. Hopefully, the breeder will be more than happy to oblige, and show you the litter in their play area.

The puppies should be in a clean, sweet-smelling, warm and comfortable environment, and they should look well fed and rounded – not pot-bellied, as this is a sure sign of worms. The litter should also appear happy, outgoing and eager to make friends with you. Before falling head over heels in love with one particular puppy, find out from the breeder which ones are available to you and try to forget the rest!

One major rule to remember is not to feel too sorry for the one that appears timid and tries to run away when the others rush forward to make friends. This puppy could well have a temperament problem which may,

what is available in the next litter. Do not go and see the puppies – you may come home with that brindle dog because you could not resist his little badger-marked face looking at you, when you really wanted an all-white bitch! It is quite possible that this puppy could turn out to be the dog of your dreams, but it is also just as possible that you may come to feel that you have been emotionally blackmailed into taking something that you did not really want.

should you give in to your urge to take him home, cause you a great deal of heartache and worry in the future.

Ideally, you want a puppy that bounds to the front, eager to be picked up and loved, and to pierce your ears for you when you do pick him up! You want a 'Gladiator of the Canine Race' – bold and fearless and not afraid of anything. This is the sort of temperament that can be built on. Nervousness is not a problem that the new Bull Terrier owner, or, for that matter, any Bull Terrier owner, wants to have to cope with.

Having been shown the whole litter together, ask the breeder if you can see those puppies which are available to you away from the rest of the litter. The breeder should be happy for you to pick up and handle the puppies, provided, of course, that you have met with any hygiene requirements that he or she may insist on. Play with the puppies, watching carefully to see if one 'chooses' you. If one does, then this is the puppy for you. Dogs have amazing instincts and quickly pick up on a character that will be compatible with their own.

Obviously, if you are looking for a show prospect, then character is not your only consideration, although it is virtually impossible, even for the most experienced breeder, to pick out a 'cert' at eight weeks of age. In order to increase your chances of finding a puppy that you can have fun with in the show ring, ask the breeder for advice, and possibly take someone with you on one of your visits who knows or has bred Bull Terriers, for additional help in choosing.

When looking at your puppy, make sure that, as well as being outgoing and well covered, he has a clear, clean coat. Run your hand against the lie of the coat to check for flea dirt, scurf or any other skin problem. Check that the ears are clean and not foul-smelling or clogged with wax. When the puppy runs around, he should move freely and without effort, showing, even at this early age, a certain amount of drive and power. Bull Terrier puppies should also carry themselves proudly. Do not worry, at this age, if their ears have not risen. Very often, a Bull Terrier puppy will lift his ears quite early, only for them to fall again while he is teething.

3 Caring For Your Bull Terrier

The Bull Terrier in general is an easily maintained breed, only asking for a well-balanced and nutritious diet, moderate exercise, moderate grooming, kind but firm handling and, most essentially, a comfortable, loving fireside home with humans to fetch and carry and to provide all a Bull Terrier could possibly require.

BEFORE THE BIG DAY

With the big day fast approaching, it is sensible to be as well prepared as possible for the arrival of your small Bull Terrier. On one of your visits to the breeder while your puppy is with his littermates, ask the breeder for information on what he or she feeds the puppies. You can then buy supplies beforehand, and not have to worry about running out of food immediately.

Other items need to be bought beforehand as well. These include bowls for both food and water, and toys especially manufactured for dogs. A small ball will not do. Too many veterinary emergencies involve young dogs and balls!

BOWLS

There is a huge variety of dog bowls on the market. However, the ideal water and food bowls are ceramic or non-rust and must be non-spill. They should also preferably be too heavy for the dog to pick up and play with. If you start with a heavy bowl, the puppy will soon get the idea that it is not a toy to be picked up and carried around, and he will look for something else to play with – hopefully one of the toys you have bought for his entertainment.

BEDS AND BEDDING

Your new Bull Terrier will also require a comfortable bed and bedding (one in the wash, one on

There is a wide selection of dog bowls to choose from, but
it is wise to opt for the heavy ceramic or stainless steel type.

The toys you buy must be both tough and safe.

A crate is an invaluable
investment – make
sure it is big enough for an
adult Bull Terrier.

the bed). Bull Terriers, although they like to squeeze into small cardboard boxes, prefer a comfortable bed to actually sleep in. The bed itself needs to be pretty durable – small puppy teeth (and, later, larger adult teeth) soon add customised frilly edges. Alternatively, a large dog crate or 'sky kennel' – big enough for an adult Bull Terrier when standing – can be obtained from good pet shops. Every dog needs his own space where he can be alone, away from the general noise and hubbub of the household, and crates provide the ideal retreat. They are also invaluable when house-training a young puppy.

You will have to decide where the new dog is going to sleep, bearing in mind that this will probably be where he sleeps for the rest of his life. Ideally, the sleeping area should be warm and draught-free, perhaps a quiet corner of the kitchen or utility area.

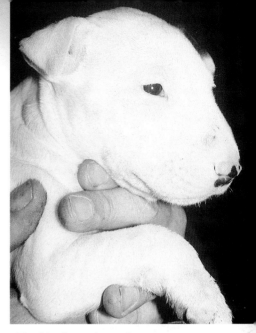

The big day arrives when you collect your puppy.

THE VET
Find a local vet and sign up. Visit and talk to the vet about the new dog, and make an appointment to take the puppy to see him or her for a health check. If at all possible, take him to the vet on your way home from the breeder. If there should be a problem that necessitates returning the puppy (fortunately, a very rare occurrence), it will be a lot easier to do if the family has not already met and fallen in love with the dog.

ON THE DAY
The big day has dawned, and you and your family will probably arrive early to pick up your new charge. However, in the excitement of collecting your new companion do not forget the paperwork.

PAPERWORK
You are entitled to expect a diet

sheet, the puppy's pedigree, and a receipt for his purchase from the breeder. You will also need the appropriate paperwork in order to register the transfer of ownership with your national kennel club.

The breeder should always provide the new owner with a diet sheet for the next stage of the puppy's development, and it is worthwhile taking this with you when you take the puppy for his first visit to the vet, so that you can discuss the feeding of the puppy.

Details of inoculations your puppy has received, if any, should be provided in the form of a certificate from the administering veterinary surgeon.

Some breeders provide their new puppy owners with short-term (generally six weeks) insurance cover, in which case you should also have a cover note included in your 'puppy pack'. If your puppy is not covered, it is advisable to ring the insurer of your choice as soon as you acquire the puppy; the first few weeks in a new home are when a puppy is most vulnerable.

You may find that the breeder will ask you to sign a contract setting out the limitations of the breeder's liability with respect to

the possibility of the puppy later developing an inheritable condition. Recent court cases have made it plain that if a breeder fails to warn a prospective purchaser of conditions that are recognised in the breed, and the puppy later develops such a condition, the breeder may be held liable, even though he or she is unaware of the existence of the problem in that puppy, and has taken what he or she considers to be all reasonable precautions to avoid the condition.

The contract you may be asked to sign must be reasonable, and is likely to consist of a statement drawing your attention to the known inheritable diseases of the breed, and an expectation that you will have discussed the significance of the condition with your veterinary surgeon.

THE JOURNEY HOME
For the journey home, it is advisable to take a companion with you and provide your new Bull Terrier with a cardboard box and an old blanket to travel home in. Place your puppy in the box on the back seat of the car, with either yourself or your companion sitting alongside to offer comfort and reassurance to the puppy. It is

Give your puppy a chance to explore his new surroundings.

also an extremely good idea to take plenty of old newspapers and kitchen roll. This is probably your puppy's first car journey, so be prepared for travel sickness and worse!

ARRIVING HOME

Although bringing a new puppy home is an important family occasion, do bear in mind that this is the first time your puppy has been away from the only surroundings he has ever known, and the world can be a big and very frightening place to a small puppy.

Try to bring your new Bull Terrier home when there are not too many people around, and introduce the puppy to his new surroundings as quietly and as gently as possible. Let him look and sniff around, offer him a little food, which he probably will not eat, and allow him to have a run around the garden to relieve himself – even if he has already done so in the car!

Bring your family and friends to meet the puppy one or two at a time, and give him time to make new friends before introducing anyone else. Remember, a puppy is like a small baby and needs plenty of sleep, particularly during a stressful time such as this, so please do not overtire the puppy by trying to do too much at once. Better to introduce people and places slowly, so that the puppy gets used to his new surroundings, than to do it all at once, and risk upsetting and confusing the poor little beast.

Once home and settled in, you should interrupt the puppy's established routine as little as possible. If you have not already bought it, the breeder may have given you a 'starter pack' of the food the puppy is used to. Even if you have decided to use a different type of food, start off by using the food the dog is used to, and follow the breeder's regime regarding the number of feeds to be given each day. Introduce any dietary changes gradually.

FEEDING
The breeder should have provided you with a diet sheet, as discussed in the last chapter. This diet sheet should not only list the number and type of meals your puppy needs to be fed now, but should also provide guidelines to feeding your pet right into adulthood. Try to stick to this diet sheet as closely as possible. If, however, you find that the regime is not fitting in with your particular routine, discuss changing it with the

breeder and your vet, and then make any changes as slowly and as gently as possible, in order not to upset your puppy's stomach. Feeding a Bull Terrier well is no great mystery, and, provided that the animal receives a well-balanced diet, it should be easy for you to find a feeding programme that suits you both.

WHEN TO FEED
When you first get your Bull Terrier puppy home, he will more than likely be requiring four meals a day, although this should be detailed in the breeder's diet sheet. By the time your Bull Terrier has reached 18 months of age, he should be able to cope with one meal a day. However, if, like many other pet owners, you feel uncomfortable about leaving your Bull Terrier apparently 'starving' for the rest of the time, it is perfectly acceptable to offer the dog a small breakfast, and feed a reduced main meal later in the day. It really does depend on your own regime and what suits you best. Once you have decided, stick to the routine. Dogs, like many other animals, are creatures of habit and do not take too kindly to having their feeding programme upset. Would you?

The advantage of a complete food is that you know your dog is getting a good-quality, balanced diet.

WHAT TO FEED

Traditionally, dogs were fed on good old meat and biscuits. However, this did not always provide a growing puppy with a balanced diet and, therefore, all kinds of supplements were advocated by breeders. Those days have long gone, and nowadays convenience and professional nutritionists combine to produce 'complete' feeds of a variety and quality that should satisfy even the fussiest of canines at every stage of life – puppy, junior, adult and senior.

It is likely that your puppy's breeder will have reared the litter on one of these 'complete' feeds, thereby making life easier and – having had the guesswork taken care of by the professionals – less worrying for you, knowing that the feed provides the puppy with all the vitamins, minerals, carbohydrates and proteins required by growing animals in one, easy-to-prepare product.

Should you decide, once you get your puppy home, to continue to use a commercial 'complete' feed, it is most important to follow the manufacturer's instructions to the letter. Too often, new owners think that they know better than the highly qualified dieticians employed by the multi-million pound pet food manufacturers, and add so-called supplements to their puppy's diet. This could cause untold damage.

There is an old saying: "If all else fails, read the instructions", and this is certainly worth bearing in mind when feeding your puppy. A heavy bowl of clean water must be provided for your puppy at all times, and is especially important if he is being fed on one of the 'complete' diets.

Bones are a contentious subject. Our Bull Terriers, both puppy and adult, certainly appreciate the large marrow-bones we give them from time to time. Large bones are not only helpful in

maintaining healthy gums and teeth, but they also provide the dog's jaws with a good workout, which may otherwise be taken on some innocent piece of furniture. However, never leave your puppy unsupervised with a bone, or give him small bones that can be swallowed, cooked bones which tend to crack or poultry bones which splinter into dangerous, sharp pieces. Likewise, we prefer not to give our dogs rawhide bones with knotted ends, as over-enthusiastic Bull Terriers have been known to chew the knots off and attempt to swallow them, which can cause choking.

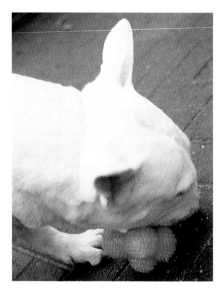

Chewing large marrow-bones is good for both teeth and gums, but never leave your dog unsupervised when he has a bone.

WHERE TO FEED

As well as deciding where your puppy is going to sleep, you must also decide where he is to eat – usually in the kitchen, and not at your dinner table. When it comes to family mealtimes, remember the puppy is at the bottom of the pack, and you should ignore his pleading face. The best solution to any attempts by the puppy to 'talk' food off your plate or to jump up at the table is to send your Bull Terrier to his bed. In time, the puppy will learn that the family dinner table is no place for him, and remain peacefully

Bull Terriers thrive on companionship and should not be left alone for long periods.

sleeping during your mealtimes, you hope!

HOUSING

Earlier, I mentioned providing your Bull Terrier puppy with a crate or sky kennel as sleeping quarters. It is not difficult to train a Bull Terrier to accept a crate – it is amazing what a little bit of bribery will do. The crate not only provides your puppy with a place of his own, where he can go to rest and be quiet, but is also an invaluable tool in house-training.

Bull Terriers would rather not be kennel dogs, although many in large establishments are. They appreciate the finer things in life far too much. Because of this, I would not advise anyone to invest in an outdoor kennel and run for just one dog. Apart from the expense, as a pack animal, a single dog does not appreciate being on his own, and may annoy your neighbours. I also think that you will rapidly find that your Bull Terrier has metamorphosed into a house dog, and the kennel has become an extra garden shed.

It is, of course, a slightly different matter if you have two or more dogs together. Although they will undoubtedly relish the time they spend in the house with you and your family, they will also enjoy themselves together, just being dogs and doing whatever it is that dogs do.

EXERCISE

Many novice Bull Terrier owners make the mistake of thinking that their young dog needs vast amounts of exercise to grow big and strong. Nothing could be further from the truth. Despite a Bull Terrier's substance, during puppyhood their bones are soft and malleable, and, consequently,

vulnerable. In order to develop properly, a young dog actually requires plenty of rest to allow for healthy growth.

For the first six months of life, a Bull Terrier puppy's exercise, other than visits to puppy parties and socialising trips, should be confined to the garden, where he can learn to accept a collar and walk on a lead in a civilised and confident manner. After this time, you can gradually introduce longer and more strenuous exercise.

BATHING

Pet Bull Terriers, particularly the coloureds, only require bathing once or twice a year, provided that they are regularly groomed. However, if they are to embark on a show career, or have developed

A play session can be more valuable than strenuous exercise.

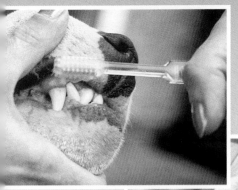

Teeth should be cleaned on a regular basis.

Nails can be clipped with guillotine type nail-clippers.

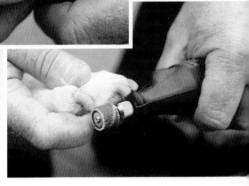

The vet may use an electric grinder for trimming nails.

the not uncommon habit of rolling in unpleasant things, then bathing is essential. It is best to get your Bull Terrier used to being bathed from an early age. If you do not, your fully-grown Bull Terrier will freak out and go into orbit the first time a shower nozzle is turned on him.

GROOMING

Although the Bull Terrier has a short, smooth coat, these dogs do benefit from regular grooming with a soft brush.

Grooming among dogs establishes and maintains the relative status of each dog within a pack. By daily grooming, you are telling your dog, in the most

Clear, sparkling eyes are an indication of good health.

gentle terms, that you are the boss. The process of making your dog stand while you brush him emphasises that, should push come to shove, you are in charge. Close handling like this not only ensures that your Bull Terrier is clean and healthy, but also prepares him for future inspections by veterinary surgeons, or perhaps even the attentions of a dog show judge.

Grooming your dog performs several important functions. The obvious one is to keep him looking and smelling acceptable to you and other people. Brushing also enables you to get to know

your puppy better, and provides an excellent opportunity to inspect him for any lumps, bumps, cuts or bruises that he may have picked up while playing. An important part of grooming involves not only brushing your Bull Terrier, but also inspecting his eyes, ears, teeth and nails on a regular basis.

EYES

Your Bull Terrier's eyes should be clear and sparkling with health, possibly with an evil glint! Although a slight, clear discharge is normal, and should be carefully removed with a damp cotton wool pad each day, there should be no cloudiness in the eye or persistent staining on the face caused by a watery discharge. You should seek veterinary advice if there are any such suspicious signs.

EARS

Ears should be checked regularly for any build-up of wax, unpleasant odours or sunburn. If wax is apparent, then it is not unreasonable to gently clean your dog's ears with cotton wool and to administer some ear-drops, as recommended by your vet. Do not dig about in your dog's ears with cotton buds or similar, as you may do some serious harm, and it will certainly be uncomfortable for your dog. Obviously, if the wax build-up persists, or if there is an unpleasant odour emanating from your dog's ears, then, again, you should seek veterinary advice.

White Bull Terriers are notorious sun-worshippers, and occasionally suffer from sunburn on the tips of their ears and nose. As with humans, prevention is better than cure, and regular daubing with a total sunblock during the summer will help to prevent the problem.

TEETH

It is advisable to get your Bull Terrier used to having his teeth looked at and cleaned (with a toothbrush and special doggie toothpaste) from an early age. There is nothing more annoying for a vet, or a judge, when trying to look at a dog's teeth, than having to battle with a 60-lb whirling dervish who has other ideas.

NAILS

A Bull Terrier's nails should be kept short. Plenty of road-walking should help to keep them in shape; however, it is necessary to cut them occasionally. Nail trimming must be started while your puppy is small and easily restrained, and is best done little and often. Trim off the very tip of the nail each time, taking care not to catch the quick. This is by far the best way of approaching the task. If, however, you cannot face doing the actual deed yourself, leave this to your vet, but do still get your Bull Terrier puppy used to having his feet and nails handled.

4 *Training*

The key to successful dog ownership is the provision of a consistent training regime from the very day you get your new Bull Terrier home. Bull Terriers possess a strong will, intelligence (although some people find this idea laughable) and a lot of charm. They also have the ability to train unprepared owners, with often disastrous consequences!

The Bull Terrier is usually amenable to training, and, to begin with, you should aim for a moderate level of obedience. This will ensure that your Bull Terrier is not only a pleasure to live with, but is also acquainted with the social graces.

CRATE-TRAINING

As well as providing your Bull Terrier with a comfortable, quiet place of his own, a crate is an invaluable aid when house-training. Firstly, you must get your puppy used to the crate.

Place the crate where you intend to keep it permanently, an area which should be both warm and draught-free. Line the crate with newspaper and place a heavy-duty cardboard box – approximately half the size of the crate – inside the crate. The front of the cardboard box should be cut out to provide easy access for your puppy. Place some durable synthetic bedding (Vetbed), toys and a small treat in the box, and leave your puppy in the box, inside the closed crate, for approximately ten minutes.

Your puppy is bound to protest loudly at being imprisoned. Do not leave, but talk to him in a soothing and reassuring manner, without touching, and soon your puppy will learn that you are not going to leave him, and that you are pleased with him. Once he has done his time, let your puppy out and make a huge fuss of him. If you persevere, your Bull Terrier

The Bull Terrier will quickly learn that a crate is his own safe haven.

will soon begin to realise that he will not be imprisoned forever, and that the crate is quite a nice place to be after all.

Once your puppy has eaten his final meal of the day, put him out into the garden and wait until he has performed. This can be quite a wait, but you will get used to this during the house-training sessions! Once the puppy has obliged, place him in his crate with a small treat and leave him there for the night. Be prepared for a long, sleepless night, but do not give in to any of his pathetic whingeing and whining, as it will only make it twice as difficult the next night.

The added advantage of using a crate as your puppy's sleeping quarters is that it helps a great deal with house-training. No dog likes to soil his own bed. If your puppy has the run of the kitchen, he will think nothing of popping out of bed, performing at the other end of the room, and retiring back to bed. However, if he has to foul just inches away from his bed, it is amazing how quickly he learns to control both bladder and bowel.

Once your puppy has learned to accept the crate, it not only provides a safe haven for him to sleep in at night, but also a useful place to keep him out of harm's way for short periods of time, such as when you have to pop to the shops for ten minutes, have 'undoggie' visitors, or simply cannot keep an eye on your young charge for a period of time.

HOUSE-TRAINING

This is the fun bit that all new puppy owners just love! The watchword here is consistency. Every morning when you get up, the first thing you must do, before even putting the kettle on, is to put your puppy outside into the garden, or wherever you have designated as his toilet. Stay with him, and once the puppy has done the necessary, make a huge fuss of him, even giving him a small treat. This little scenario has to be played out, come rain or shine, after every one of your puppy's meals, every time he wakes up and last thing at night before retiring to bed. If you get into this habit, then your Bull Terrier will soon learn to be 'clean'.

Obviously, during the night the crate will help enormously. However, there will be the odd occasion when your puppy has an 'accident'. If this happens in your presence, then a reprimand, in the form of a firm "No", and placing the puppy immediately in the designated toilet area will soon bring the message home. If, however, the 'accident' has occurred some time before, there is absolutely no point in chastising your puppy. He simply will not know what he is being told off for and assume it is because of what he is doing at the present time, which could quite easily be sleeping peacefully in his crate.

COLLAR AND LEAD TRAINING

It is advisable to accustom your new Bull Terrier to wearing a collar, and walking on a lead, from an early age. Once he is old enough to venture out into the big wide world, he will have to be on a lead at all times and wear a collar bearing your home telephone number.

To begin with, place a soft leather or nylon collar around your puppy's neck just before starting a game. Although he should not be unduly worried by the collar – the puppy may scratch as if he had an itch – the game will soon grab his attention, and all else will be forgotten. Follow this procedure each day, and your puppy will soon get used to the feel of the collar touching his neck.

The next step is to introduce the lead by attaching it to the puppy's collar in the usual manner and letting him drag the lead around with him during his games. Once your puppy is used to the feel of the lead then you

Your puppy will soon become a strong, powerful adult, so it is important to establish good manners on the lead at an early age.

can begin to hold it. Pick up the lead and walk with your puppy round the garden, telling him to "Heel". As soon as your puppy starts to protest or pull, simply stop and encourage him to come to you with praise and a small tidbit. Do not have a tug-of-war. Once your puppy comes to you, start to walk round the garden again, making full use of bribery. Remember the donkey and the carrot?

These sessions should be short and repeated frequently. In this way, you can teach your dog to walk on the lead in a civilised way, without pulling.

However, there may come a time when your small Bull Terrier decides to challenge the idea of being restrained by the lead and tries an experimental pull to see what happens. Do not do what so many dog owners seem to do, and return the pull, because this will cause all your hard work to go out of the window. Your puppy learns that the normal thing to do is lean into his lead and pull his owner around behind him. Instead, rather than letting the pull become established, without letting go of the lead, call your puppy back to you immediately, and stop walking (or even walk in the opposite direction). Praise your puppy and even offer a bribe when he comes back. Start again, and keep him on a very short lead so that he cannot move out ahead of you. Remember, in doggie society the top dog walks ahead. Who is top dog in your family?

Once your puppy has got fully used to walking on his collar and lead, then, and only then, can he be introduced to the outside world.

THE OUTSIDE WORLD

Once your puppy is used to his collar and lead and has had his final vaccinations, it is time to start to introduce him to the outside world. It is quite a good idea to take your puppy with you, if possible, when you go shopping or on family outings. In this way, your puppy will meet more people and see strange sights that he would not see at home. These initial trips should be short and sweet, and will not only introduce your puppy to new experiences but also get him used to travelling in the car.

While out on these socialising trips, if your puppy shows any sign of fear at any object or situation he encounters, take time to familiarise him with the problem. A great deal of patience and calmness is called for in order to avoid putting your puppy under any unnecessary pressure and to allay the fear successfully. Your puppy must learn to have complete trust in you and learn that no harm will come to him while you are around.

SOCIALISING

It has been scientifically proven that a dog's greatest potential for learning occurs between the ages of six weeks and four months. It is also fair to say that early experiences have an enormous impact on a puppy's development, and leave lifelong impressions. Therefore, it is most important that all your young puppy's experiences are pleasant ones.

All young puppies need to meet as many other dogs and humans as possible. This is the essence of socialisation, and when done effectively, will help to avoid many of the behavioural problems that may otherwise occur later.

From the day you bring your new puppy home, he should start to meet other people. The puppy

Try to get your puppy used to as many new situations as possible during the vital learning period.

must not be overwhelmed, but, within reason, the more people he meets, the better. Obviously, until your puppy has received his vaccinations, some caution is necessary in order to avoid 'second-hand' contact with possibly sick dogs, by asking their owners to delay their visit until your puppy has had his second injections.

Your visitors should be asked to hold the puppy, or to gently handle him, so that the puppy learns that people are friends.

Apart from other dogs in the household, to whom your puppy should be introduced at the earliest possible moment, meeting dogs must be delayed until the puppy has had the all-clear from your veterinary surgeon at about twelve weeks of age.

One of the most useful developments in puppy training in recent years has been the creation of 'puppy parties'. These are exactly as they sound. Once or twice a week, a group of puppy owners with their small charges meet for an hour or so in a local hall. Puppies aged from twelve weeks to six or seven months, of all shapes and sizes, are then allowed to play with each other, with the minimum of restraint from their owners. The smallest are rarely overwhelmed by their larger cousins – more often, quite the reverse – and all learn that their fellow canines can be approached without fear.

The puppy party has revolutionised dog training. Most puppy groups have an experienced trainer in charge, and the transition from pure play to early obedience training can be effortless.

BASIC OBEDIENCE

Once your puppy walks to heel on a loose lead, and responds to your command to heel with reasonable alacrity, you are well on your way to having an obedient Bull Terrier.

Teaching a puppy to 'sit' on command, and to 'down' are the next steps, with practical uses for any dog.

With the essentials – patience, praise and bribery – it should be a relatively simple exercise to teach your Bull Terrier to sit. Restrain your puppy in a standing position, using a lead that is sufficiently short to prevent him from jumping up to reach the bribe. Move the tidbit from in front of the puppy, over his head, to just behind his head. Usually, your puppy will sit and tip his head back to try to reach the titbit. Praise your puppy and give him the sweet, and in one quick, easy session you have taught your puppy to sit. Repeat the exercise, this time telling your puppy to "Sit" as you do so, and keep doing it until your puppy has learnt that "Sit" means 'sit for a sweet'.

The next step is to teach the 'down' as an extension of the same exercise. Once your puppy has learned the 'sit', and while

Bull Terriers love their food, so teaching basic obedience with the aid of a titbit makes good sense.

keeping him under the same restraint, offer the sweet on the floor between his front legs, and push the puppy down at the same time, telling him to "Down". The 'down' is possibly one of the most useful obedience exercises to teach your Bull Terrier. If ever you find yourself and your dog in an emergency situation, a quick response to the "Down" command could be a life-saver.

Elementary obedience lessons do not need skilled assistance, but even these can contain pitfalls for the new owner. However, help can always be sought from the local dog training or obedience class. There are many of these classes up and down the country, and they are well worth joining. Most classes are run by experienced dog owners, who are only too happy to pass on their knowledge to novices. These obedience groups all have classes for beginners – both dogs and owners. A well-trained house pet is the objective.

SHOW TRAINING

If you bought your young Bull Terrier with showing in mind and he matures into a good example of the breed, you may wish to try showing him. However, before taking the plunge, a little 'ringcraft' training is called for in order to avoid potential embarrassment.

Showing a Bull Terrier is a relatively simple exercise as you do not have to 'stack' the dog (that is, place his feet in position and hold his head and tail up) in the same way as with other breeds. However, you do need to teach your puppy to walk in a straight line on a loose lead, pose with his ears up (looking intelligent!) and stand while he is examined closely by a judge, all in the close proximity of other dogs. This examination by the judge includes an inspection of your animal's teeth, head, the rest of his body, and, in the case of male dogs, the testicles. From an early age your puppy must get used to strangers handling him all over.

To 'stand' your Bull Terrier, walk him into position. He should stand four-square, with his weight evenly balanced on all four feet. The Bull Terrier's expression should be attentive and alert, with his ears up – attract your dog's attention with a favourite toy or treat, if necessary. Your dog should also stand happily on a loose lead, as a Bull Terrier's neck and shoulders look far better with the lead laid low rather than held tightly behind the ears. When practising at home, ask a neighbour or friend that the dog does not know well to go over him, checking his mouth and handling him all over.

The next step is to move your Bull Terrier as if you were in the show ring. Moving your Bull Terrier on a loose lead is really

The aim of show training is for the dog to walk into show pose, stand four-square, and look bright and intelligent awaiting the judge's inspection.

just an extension of his lead training. However, it is vitally important that your dog learns to move, without pulling, in a triangle, a circle and straight up and down. Your Bull Terrier then needs to stand, again on a loose lead, for a final appraisal by the judge.

Again, these sessions should be short and repeated frequently. Your puppy should think of this presentation work as a fun game and enjoy it greatly. With plenty of praise and lots of treats, almost all Bull Terriers will learn the skills required for showing.

Ring Training classes are extremely helpful to the novice, and are run in much the same way as the obedience classes, but are intended specifically to produce well-trained show dogs.

The emphasis is on good behaviour on the lead, in the presence of other dogs and a crowd of people, training the dog to allow strangers to examine him, and to 'stand' while on the lead rather than sit.

5 *Showing Your Bull Terrier*

Before embarking on a show career with your Bull Terrier, you must first decide whether he or she is really good enough to show, and it is imperative that you be brutally honest with yourself.

Talk to your puppy's breeder, and, if possible, take your puppy along for an assessment. If the breeder tells you that your dog has developed into an animal worth showing, then go for it, but do not run before you can walk. Start at small local shows, where you and your puppy can gain confidence and learn the ropes, before progressing to the major shows, where you will be up against some of the best dogs in the country, competing for top honours.

Shows are, in general, great fun for both dog and owner. You both get to meet new friends and share a common interest. However, once you have decided to put your Bull Terrier up against his rivals, you must be prepared to take the rough with the smooth. There is no such thing as the perfect Bull Terrier; even the top Champions have some minor fault or two. If you can appreciate that your precious Bull Terrier is less than perfect and can cope with a judge's constructive criticism, then showing your dog could become a pleasurable and relatively inexpensive hobby.

Remember, too, at the end of the show, win or lose, you have chosen your particular dog because you wanted him as a pet and companion. If you remember this, then you will always be taking the best dog home with you.

To give you an idea of what a judge is looking for when judging Bull Terriers, it would probably help to read the Breed Standard.

THE BREED STANDARD
All pedigree dogs have a Breed

Standard – a blueprint against which all judges should assess competitors. This blueprint details, step-by-step, what constitutes the perfect Bull Terrier in a show, and your dog will be measured against this, and then assessed alongside the competition in its class.

OVERALL IMPRESSION

To begin with, the judge will look at all the dogs in the class and get an overall impression of their appearance.

The Bull Terrier, both dog and bitch, must have the typical egg-shaped head – without this, it is simply not a Bull Terrier. The animal should also give the impression of being a well-balanced, strongly-built, muscular and active dog, and have a keen, determined and intelligent expression, displaying an interest in the surroundings and fellow competitors without being temperamental or undisciplined. Irrespective of size, dogs should look masculine, and bitches feminine.

The Bull Terrier should be strongly-built, with a keen determined impression. This is Ch. White Voodoo of Kilacabar.

The unique egg-shaped head is a feature of the breed.
This is Ch. Denpower Baron Of Bullydale.

HEAD

The Bull Terrier's egg-shaped head is what sets him apart from every other breed. Because of this, Bull Terriers are often referred to as a 'head breed'. If an animal appears in the ring who does not have a typical Bull Terrier head, then no matter how sound he is, he is not a good Bull Terrier, and should therefore be penalised accordingly.

A good head is long, strong and deep, right to the end of the muzzle. It should display a gently curved profile that starts between the ears and flows down to the tip of the nose, which should always be black and bent downwards at the tip. When viewed from the front, the head appears to be egg-shaped and completely filled – no hollows or indentations. The skull between the ears is flat and not domed. The face should be filled with bone, particularly under the eyes, giving the head a look of considerable strength.

There should be no coarseness or lippiness and the head should be in proportion to the rest of the dog.

MOUTH

Contained in a strong, square muzzle, with a strong and deep under-jaw, the Bull Terrier's teeth should be clean, large, strong and display a regular and complete scissor-bite, set square to the jaws. This means that his top teeth should fit neatly over the bottom, enabling the dog to use his teeth in the same manner as a pair of scissors.

Three faults that may be in Bull Terrier mouths are: 'undershot' – where the lower teeth or under-jaw protrude beyond the upper teeth and jaw; 'overshot' – vice versa; and 'inset canines', which often occur when the dog has a narrow under-jaw. The dog's lower canine teeth appear to be set inside the lower jaw and often interfere with the roof of the dog's mouth. All three faults are highly undesirable.

EYES
A Bull Terrier's eyes give the impression of being small. This is due to the shape and size of the opening, which should be narrow, triangular and set at an angle, with the corner of the lower eyelid pointing towards the outer corner of the ear. The eye itself is deep-set and should be black or as dark brown as possible. Despite being so deep-set, a Bull Terrier's eyes are most expressive, usually displaying a wicked sense of humour.

EARS
A Bull Terrier looks his most intelligent and alert when his ears, which should be small and thin, are placed close together on the top of his head and held erect. Those Bull Terriers with ears set down the sides of their skull at 'ten to two' generally look less alert, dopey even, as the ears give the impression of being too large.

NECK
The neck should be muscular, long and arched, widening from

The forelegs are strong with good-quality bone.

the dog's head to his shoulders. It should also be 'clean', showing no loose skin.

FOREQUARTERS

A Bull Terrier's neck should flow into strong and muscular shoulders. The shoulder blades, which should be wide, flat and held closely to the chest wall, should show a pronounced backward slope of the front edge

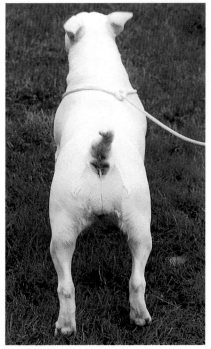

The hindquarters should be muscular – they provide the power when the dog is moving.

from bottom to top, forming what looks like a right angle with the dog's upper arm. The elbows must be held close to the dog's body, although they should not be so close as to be called 'tied in at the elbow'. Neither should they stick out like a Bulldog's.

The forelegs on the Bull Terrier are well muscled, with strong, round, quality bone and upright pasterns. When viewed from the front, the forelegs should be perfectly parallel and the chest broad and straight.

HINDQUARTERS

A Bull Terrier's hindquarters provide the power during movement. Therefore, he requires muscular thighs, well-developed second thighs, a well-bent stifle and well-angulated hock joints. When viewed from behind, the hindlegs should be parallel and the hock joints themselves should be close to the ground – a 'well-let-down hock'.

BODY

The Bull Terrier's body should be well rounded (not fat), with a well-sprung ribcage. He should show great depth from his withers to his brisket, providing heart and lung room, and also display a

The body is rounded with a well-sprung ribcage This is Ch. Arcanum Kalamkari.

good forechest. His back should be short, strong and level, only arching slightly over well-muscled loins.

FEET
The Bull Terrier actually has quite small, round and compact feet. They should not be flat or splayed, but have well-arched toes and hard, thick pads.

TAIL
The Bull Terrier's tail should be short, set on low and carried horizontally in the show ring. It should be thick at the root, tapering towards the tip.

MOVEMENT
When moving, the Bull Terrier should give the impression that it is covering the ground with free, easy strides in a typically jaunty Bull Terrier fashion. When viewed from the side, the Bull Terrier's forelegs should reach out well and its hindlegs – moving smoothly from the hip and flexing well at the stifle and hock – should drive the dog forward with great thrust. Movement should be parallel

when viewed from both front and back.

COLOUR

Bull Terriers come in a variety of colours – white, brindle, black brindle, tricolour, red, fawn. All these colours are allowed in the show ring, although tick markings (black flecks) in white coats, and blue or liver dogs, are highly undesirable.

COAT

A Bull Terrier's coat is short, flat, even and harsh to the touch. It should also have a fine gloss, although this is not as easy to see on the whites as it is on the coloureds. Its skin should be tight-fitting without any spare folds anywhere.

SIZE

There is no mention of size or weight in the Bull Terrier Breed Standard. What it does say, however, is that the Bull Terrier must give the impression of maximum substance for size of dog, consistent with quality and sex.

TYPES OF SHOW

Once you have decided to show your Bull Terrier, you will need to find the shows in which you can enter him. It is far better to start at the bottom of the ladder before gradually working your way up as your puppy wins. The types of show, and the classes, vary from country to country, so contact your national kennel club for details.

PRESENTATION

When showing your Bull Terrier, it is advisable to turn him, and yourself, out to the best of your ability. This means bathing and trimming your dog, and turning yourself out in neat and tidy clothes in order to do justice to your dog.

White Bull Terriers should be bathed the day before the show, to turn what is usually a grubby grey dog into a sparkling white vision. One trick to improve whiteness is to brush chalk into your dog's coat while it is still slightly damp. In accordance with Kennel Club rules, this should be brushed out before entering the show ring.

Coloured dogs do not require the same amount of bathing, usually only needing a quick wipe-over with a sponge or a chamois. However, if your dog's white bits are grubby, these will

BULL TERRIER COLOURS

The classic white Bull Terrier.

White and brindle.

Red and white.

Black, white and brindle.

certainly need to be washed. Bath coloured dogs two or three days before the show in order to let the coat settle, as, occasionally, bathing can cause scurf to rise, and turn a smart, shiny, black brindle into every anti-dandruff shampoo advertiser's dream.

When it comes to trimming a Bull Terrier's hair, there is not a great deal to do, but it is amazing what a difference a little snipping makes to the appearance of your dog.

All Bull Terriers have what are fondly termed 'ratty whiskers'. Bull Terriers do not produce long wispy whiskers, but, rather, short, stubby and curly affairs that cling to the dog's face, producing a slightly fuzzy outline. Judicious trimming, with curved scissors, of the whiskers around your Bull Terrier's mouth, eyebrows and chin will smooth the outline.

The Breed Standard calls for a tail that is short, thick at the root and tapering to a fine point. Therefore, you may find it necessary to trim the underside of your Bull Terrier's tail with a thinning knife, and also take the pointed tip of hair off the end with a pair of curved scissors. Trimming your Bull Terrier is an art and needs a steady hand and

nerve. If you are unsure of your trimming skills, ask for help from other Bull Terrier owners who are always willing to help a novice.

Last, but not least, consider your own attire. After all that hard work, training, bathing and trimming your dog and turning him out beautifully, why spoil the whole effect by wearing scruffy jeans and a tatty T-shirt? If you are well turned out it complements the appearance of your dog and presents a pleasant overall picture of dog and owner in harmony.

Try to be relaxed when showing your dog, as nerves tend to travel down the lead.

EQUIPMENT

When attending dog shows, you must remember to put the following items in your show bag:

Show lead (clean, thin, white rope, slip variety)

Grooming mitt

Chamois leather and coat dressing (for coloured dogs)

Chalk (that you must brush out before entering the ring)

Bag of tidbits and your dog's favourite toy

Benching chain and blanket (if the show is benched)

Crate and blanket (if the show is not benched)

Ring clip for holding your number

Poop scoop and disposal bags (for cleaning up after your dog)

Bottle of drinking water and bowl (many dogs will not drink strange water)

Towel or towelling coat (to keep your dog cool on a hot day)

Coat (to keep your dog warm on a cold day).

AT THE SHOW

On the day of the show, aim to arrive at least half an hour before judging is due to start. This will enable you to get into the showground and get your dog settled without getting too flustered. Offer your dog a little water and then walk him around to get him used to the strange sights and sounds and relieve himself. Place your dog back on his bench or in his crate. Ask a friend to keep an eye on your dog and go and buy a catalogue to check that your dog has been entered into the correct class. If he is not, contact the secretary.

Return to your dog and, if necessary, exercise him again. As the class prior to yours goes in, give your Bull Terrier a quick going-over to check for any

The judge assesses each Bull Terrier against the Breed Standard, and decides which dog, on the day, comes closest to the ideal.

recently acquired dirty marks. Put on his show lead and arrive at the ringside in good time, ready to enter when the steward calls your class. If it is an Open show, you will get your ring number from the steward; if it is a Championship show, remember to pick it up from your bench. Stand where the steward requests and pose your dog, remembering to talk to him all the time – it will settle your nerves just as much as his.

When the judge goes over your Bull Terrier, you may be asked a few questions. Please do remember that it is not the done thing to engage a judge in conversation – only speak when you are spoken to. Be certain to follow the judge's requests – a judge asks you to move your dog in a certain way in order to assess him. If you do not move your dog correctly, you may be damaging his chances.

As the last dog in your class is being assessed, attract your Bull Terrier's attention and get him standing correctly. Try to keep one eye on your dog and one on the judge. If you are fortunate

enough to be pulled out, stand where the judge or steward asks you to. Do not assume that this is the final placing as your dog may be asked to move again before any decisions are made. If you receive a prize card, a polite thank-you to the judge and steward will not go amiss. Congratulations to those placed above you also creates a good impression.

If you are lucky enough to have won your class, then your dog or bitch is considered 'unbeaten' and, unless entered in any subsequent classes and beaten, it is eligible to challenge for Best Dog, Best Bitch or Best of Breed. If you should win Best of Breed, then it can only be courteous to the judge and good for the breed to stay for the Best in Show or Group competition.

As I have said before, showing is an enjoyable hobby. Win or lose, remember that the Bull Terrier you are taking home with you is the one you chose to be your friend and companion. He is the same dog you left for the show with that morning, and you are still taking the best dog home with you.

6 *Breeding*

There are all too many reasons for not breeding from your Bull Terrier bitch. Most of these occupy Bull Terrier welfare kennels!

Breeding Bull Terriers should not be undertaken on a whim. It requires knowledge of the breed and demands total dedication, and a great deal of hard work.

Even if you think you have the necessary expertise and dedication, do you have a good enough dog or bitch? There is no truth in the belief that siring a litter will in any way 'settle a dog down'. Neither is there any truth in the belief that a bitch 'needs to have a litter'. There are many happy, healthy Bull Terriers up and down the country, all leading perfectly normal lives, in blissful ignorance of the reproductive process.

In reality, unless your Bull Terrier dog has taken the show world by storm, it is highly unlikely that even occasional stud work will come his way. Likewise, even if your bitch is a top prizewinner, if you cannot guarantee several good homes for her puppies, then do not even consider mating her. If you want to sustain family continuity after she has died, then return to her breeder.

Other considerations to be taken into account before embarking on breeding a litter of Bull Terriers include: cost, available space, disruption to routines and coping with the mess created by small Bull Terriers intent on causing mayhem.

THE RIGHT STUD DOG

Once you have made up your mind that you are going to breed from your Bull Terrier bitch and it has been confirmed, preferably by her breeder, that she is suitable, then you will need to find a suitable stud dog for her.

When considering a suitable

Think carefully before planning to breed a litter.

stud dog for your bitch, take into account her qualities, and select a dog that will prove to be of the greatest worth to her.

Do not always go to the most fashionable stud dog for your bitch's mating. Take advice. An experienced breeder will be able to advise you which dog is right for your bitch, using both the physical appearance of your bitch and the available dogs and the pedigree of both. Some breeders take more notice of pedigree, others of conformation. Learn about the breed, and decide how close to your ideal Bull Terrier each breeder's stock is.

Once you have decided upon a potential stud dog, it is more than likely that his owner will want to assess your bitch before committing to the mating. The dog's owner may well refuse the mating if he or she considers the two dogs incompatible. After all, there is a stud dog's reputation to keep. If, however, both parties agree to the mating, then a stud fee will be negotiated.

The better (or more fashionable) the stud dog, the higher the fee. As a guide, the stud fee is likely to be somewhat lower than the price you might expect to receive for the sale of a puppy.

Mother (left) and son: A lot of planning goes into developing a breeding programme.

The stud dog owners may like the look of your bitch, and think that the mating could produce something good. In this case, they may suggest they have 'pick of litter', which means that they have the right to pick whichever they regard as the best puppy from the litter, either in lieu of the stud fee, or as a consideration for a reduced fee. If you make this sort of arrangement, do make sure that the details are put down in writing.

KENNEL CLUB AFFIX

Pedigree dogs registered with the Kennel Club usually have, as part of their registered name, their breeder's 'affix' or kennel name. If you breed a litter, you may wish to register your own affix so that all your puppies carry your own unique identification. To apply for an affix, you will need to complete a special form from the Kennel Club, and you will probably have to submit several choices. Remember to put your preferred choice first!

Affixes are chosen in various ways – a combination of the owners' names, house names, a play on words or something relating to their foundation bitch. Choosing an affix can be

BREEDING

tremendous fun, but remember that your puppies' registered names are only allowed a maximum of 24 letters – including the affix!

MATING AND CONCEPTION

True oestrus begins at about twelve days from the first signs of your bitch coming into season. From that time, she will be fertile for five to seven days, and accept the stud dog's attempts to mate her. Ovulation – the release of eggs into the uterus – takes place during this period. The timing is variable, and the dog and bitch are the best practical arbiters of the bitch's fertile period, although laboratory tests are available to help with timing if the bitch fails to conceive.

The mating act may be prolonged. Once the dog has ejaculated, the bitch continues to grip his penis in her vagina, by means of a ring of muscle, for up to twenty minutes. The dog may climb off the bitch's back, and both stand 'tied' – tail to tail. The tie is not actually essential for a successful mating, although all breeders prefer to see it.

Following the mating, the stud dog owner will give you a copy of the stud dog's pedigree and a signed form for the Kennel Club registration of the puppies, which certifies that the mating took place, and with their consent.

PREPARING FOR WHELPING

Pregnant bitches do not need to be crammed full of the latest additives. As long as they receive a well-balanced diet, they should have nothing more than a slightly increased food intake during the last few weeks of pregnancy. As the bitch's girth increases, she may well prefer to have her food ration divided into two or three.

Let your veterinary surgeon know well in advance. He or she

You must be confident that your bitch is a good specimen of the breed, as well as being sound in mind and body.

61

In most cases whelping should be straightforward, and the bitch will cope well with her new duties.

may actually have confirmed that the bitch is in whelp, but ask them to note the expected date on their calendar.

Make sure that you have decided where the bitch is to whelp, and that she is in agreement with you. If it is to be in a special place, in a special bed, introduce her to it a week or two in advance, and teach her that it is now her bed. The ideal place is a quiet corner without passing traffic, but do bear in mind that you, or the vet, may have to attend to her at some stage, so under the stairs may not be perfect!

Your bitch should have a whelping box, which needs to be large, to accommodate both the bitch and the litter. Most breeders will show you a suitable pattern of box, probably with a 'pig' rail around the edge to prevent the bitch overlaying her puppies. Bedding for the box needs to be disposable, as whelping is accompanied by a great deal of mess. It is almost universally accepted that the basic bedding for a whelping box is newspaper – in large quantities – so start saving several weeks' worth in advance of the big day.

WHELPING

Whelping is a natural event, and in most cases there is no need for human interference. In ninety-nine cases out of a hundred, interference takes place before it is really necessary.

Most bitches give a warning of imminent whelping by going off their food. Their temperature also drops by two to three degrees, which is nearly always an indication that the bitch will start to whelp within 24 hours.

For several days prior to whelping, many bitches will start nesting, usually somewhere totally inappropriate, like in the middle of your bed! Most bitches become very restless a few hours before they start to whelp.

It may take several hours from the time the bitch starts to strain until the first puppy is delivered. Provided that she continues to strain, there is no panic. If, however, after serious effort for an hour or more, she stops trying, seek advice from your veterinary surgeon.

The first sign that a puppy is due is the appearance of the 'water bag', an apt description for the foetal membranes; they look just like a small bag of water which appears through the vagina.

Do not attempt to remove this, as its function is to enlarge the birth canal to permit the following puppy to pass through.

The puppy may be born either head or tail first – both are equally common, and the appearance of the tail first does not indicate a 'breech birth'.

Once the puppy has emerged, gently remove the membrane from around the puppy, paying particular attention to the face and mouth, and place it at the bitch's head so that she can clean and dry the puppy, sever the umbilical cord and eat the afterbirth. Should the bitch have a problem with biting the umbilical cord, you can tie it with some catgut a little way from the puppy's body, and cut the cord with sterilised scissors.

Once the bitch has cleaned up her puppy, try to 'button' it on to a teat and encourage it to suckle. Follow this procedure with each puppy.

At the end of a normal whelping, your Bull Terrier bitch should be a tired but extremely proud mother. At this stage, it is probably advisable to ask your vet to check her over to ensure that there are no more puppies lurking inside. Once all the puppies have been born and are suckling happily, leave the new family for a while. After about half an hour, encourage your bitch to leave her babies and go outside to relieve herself.

While she is out of the way, place the puppies on to a clean piece of bedding (such as Vetbed) in a box, and remove the newspapers from the whelping box. Clean and dry out the whelping box, put in a clean layer of newspapers and yet more clean bedding – your washing machine will not thank you for having a litter of puppies in the house! Put the puppies back into the whelping box and let their mother back in. Once she has settled herself and her family, offer her a drink of glucose and water and perhaps even a small, light meal of scrambled eggs.

Most Bull Terrier bitches make excellent mothers. Occasionally, they may be a little clumsy or rough with their puppies, particularly if they are new mothers. This usually occurs when they are rushing back in from relieving themselves and are anxious that someone may have taken their brood. Normally, the bitch is left constantly with her puppies for at least the first couple of weeks, and you may have difficulty in persuading her to leave them, even to relieve herself. If this is the case, do not worry. She will go eventually!

WHELPING PROBLEMS

The first puppy may take some time to be born from the time you get the first sight of it, and may often seem to disappear back up the birth canal. The time for concern is when the puppy appears to be stuck fast with no movement up or down, despite continued straining, or when the bitch appears to have given up straining and is lying exhausted. Veterinary attention must be sought urgently, and in all probability a Caesarean section performed.

Caesareans are more popular nowadays partly because of humane considerations, but of great importance is the existence of very low-risk anaesthetics and improved surgical techniques. A successful outcome – live puppies and a healthily recovering bitch – can usually be anticipated these days, but the operation must be carried out sooner rather than later. The subject should be discussed with your veterinary surgeon well before the whelping

For the first few weeks, the time is divided between eating and sleeping.

is due, so that you are both aware of the other's feelings about it. The vet must be called in before the bitch has become exhausted from straining unsuccessfully.

Caesarean operations must be carried out with the facilities of the surgery's operating theatre, and for this reason most vets will ask you to bring the bitch to the surgery if there seem to be any whelping difficulties.

The bitch involved in a Caesarean is, almost by definition, otherwise healthy, and with her puppies, will thrive best back in her home environment. The vet will usually let her and her puppies be taken home as soon as possible.

Once home, she may need a little coaxing to accept and feed the puppies; as far as she is concerned, they just appeared while she was asleep.

Careful introductions almost always work, but she may need some help initially to 'button on' the puppies. Once they are suckling normally, the bitch will realise what it is all about.

THE NEW FAMILY

A healthy bitch with puppies quickly develops a large appetite. For the first few days, it may be necessary to feed her in, or very close to, her bed, but make sure there is plenty of food available, and particularly plenty of fluids. Forget the once-a-day feeding regime and let the bitch have food whenever she wants it. After all, she has an enormous task ahead of her.

Your bitch will continue to discharge a heavy, bloody fluid for several days after the whelping. If this discharge becomes bright red in colour – or foul-smelling, seek

PUPPY WATCHING

By four weeks of age, the puppies are becoming increasingly active.

veterinary attention immediately as this could be an indication of a life-threatening womb infection.

Regularly check your bitch's teats for any small lumps, which may indicate the start of mastitis. If you do feel any lumps, ask your vet to check her as well, as a course of antibiotics may be required.

The first two weeks are the easiest, because during this time the puppies are relatively motionless. They will wriggle around a great deal, but are incapable of returning to the nest should they fall out. It is to stop the puppies falling or climbing out that most whelping boxes have high fronts. At this stage, the puppies need no supplementary feeding and should spend most of their time sleeping peacefully. If they do not, seek help, urgently.

Bull Terrier puppies first open their eyes at about ten days old. By the time they reach three weeks, they are moving around more, and it is highly likely that every one has fallen out of the whelping box on more than one occasion. If this is the case, add another layer to the barrier at the front.

Bull Terrier puppies grow at a tremendous rate – as do their toe-nails. These nails may be small, but can become extremely sharp if not trimmed regularly. Trimming your litter's nails is a relatively simple task. When the puppies are tiny, use a pair of human nail-clippers, advancing to dog nail-clippers as the puppies, and their feet, get larger.

WEANING

Weaning can begin when the puppies are aged around three to four weeks of age. Although most people think of the first hand-feeding of puppies as an occasion for something delicate, milky perhaps, just try scraping a little raw beef on to your fingers. With Bull Terrier puppies you will be lucky to have a finger left! It is also at this age that the litter must have their first worming dose.

From three weeks to about five weeks of age, a gradually increasing proportion of the puppies' diet should be supplied from sources other than their mother's milk. To begin, introduce the puppies to other foods very gradually – half a teaspoon of scraped raw beef or purpose-made puppy food on your finger is plenty. Once the puppies have become interested, you can increase the amount you

Weaning is well underway, but the puppies will continue to feed from their mother for as long as she will tolerate them.

The puppies will learn through playing together and exploring their environment.

As the breeder, it is your responsibility to find good homes for the puppies.

give them. Within reason, a puppy should be allowed to eat as much as he wants, and most proprietary foods provide a feeding guide on the packet. Your puppies will soon learn to eat from a bowl, and it is up to you whether you prefer to feed them from one large bowl or from several individual ones. In general, breeders tend to feed their puppies two meat meals and two milk-based meals per day.

By six weeks of age, the puppies should be completely weaned – although their mother may take some convincing of this. They should be feeding on a puppy food of your choice, and it is also time for a second worming.

NEW HOMES

The most important consideration when breeding a litter of Bull Terriers is finding good homes for them. You will have reared the puppies with love and care, and must ensure that they go to homes where they will be looked after just as well.

If you do not have firm orders to ensure the sale of all of your puppies, the breeder of your bitch may be able to help. Good puppies are at a premium, and breeders with good reputations receive regular phone calls from prospective buyers, enquiring about the availability of puppies. Your bitch's breeder may be one of these breeders, and be happy to pass on applicants to you.

It is often a bitter-sweet occasion when the puppies go off to their new homes. However, in the coming months and years, it is hoped that their new owners will continue to keep you in touch with what their Bull Terrier is up to. Remember, also, that you, as the breeder, have a responsibility to those puppies and their owners. As such, you should always be prepared to offer them support.

7 Health Care

In general, Bull Terriers are a pretty hardy breed. However, as with every breed, they do need routine maintenance in order to remain healthy and happy. During your regular grooming sessions, you should check your dog's eyes, ears, teeth and coat, as described in Chapter Three. If your dog seems off-colour or off his food, and you are in any doubt whatsoever, contact your vet immediately. The vet is the professional, and in times of trouble he or she is you and your dog's best friend.

INOCULATIONS

It is essential that your Bull Terrier puppy is inoculated against distemper (which includes hardpad), leptospirosis (a liver and kidney infection), hepatitis (caused by a liver virus) and parvovirus. Kennel cough vaccines may also be included at this primary vaccination stage.

The usual routine is for the initial vaccine to be given at approximately eight weeks of age, followed by a second injection at twelve weeks. The inoculations are then repeated annually and this is known as the 'booster'.

Owners tend to lapse in their response to booster reminders from their vet as their dog gets older. Beware! Although some elements of the vaccination programme may provide your dog with immunity for life, this cannot be relied on, and other elements most definitely need boosting each year.

PARASITES

WORMS
When you buy your puppy, the breeder should advise you of the puppy's worming treatment up to that time. Virtually all puppies are born with internal worms –

ascarids. A proper rearing regime will include dosing the litter when it is three or four weeks of age, and perhaps again prior to leaving the kennels. Once in your home, the puppy should be treated regularly, according to your veterinary surgeon's advice, but most probably once a month until he is six months old. Modern worm medicines have no side effects, and would appear to be reasonably palatable, although some dogs take some convincing of this. More importantly, the ascarid roundworm may be the cause of a rare eye condition in children. If your dog is regularly wormed, the risk, which is already remote, is eliminated.

Roundworms are not always easy to detect in a dog's faeces, but, in puppies, it is safe to assume that they are present.

Tapeworms are less common, but are still seen regularly. They are usually transmitted by the dreaded flea. Treatment is, again, simple, but should be combined with a determined effort to get rid of any fleas. Tapeworms may be recognised as 'rice grains' in the faeces, but your puppy may give you an indication by paying undue attention to his anal region.

FLEAS

Fleas are by far the commonest external parasite of the dog, and a high proportion of skin problems may be caused, directly or indirectly, by their presence.

Although your puppy should be free of fleas when you collect him from the breeder, fleas are extremely common and are easily picked up, although not so easily seen on a dog. It is always best to assume that at some time your puppy may have fleas, particularly if he becomes itchy, seems to have small bites on his skin or appears to have 'coal dust' in his coat.

Fleas thrive in the warm environment of the modern home, and, with central heating, there no longer appears to be a 'flea season' in summer followed by a relatively flea-free winter. Therefore, treatment really needs to be carried out all year round.

Flea control is a matter of continued vigilance, both in treating your dog and your home. Thankfully, there are now a number of effective spray-on treatments for dogs, as well as useful tablet formulations designed to prevent fleas from breeding.

The important thing to remember, however, is that fleas leave their host to reproduce, and that for every flea you find on your dog, there are another thousand, quite literally, in your dog's bed and in your carpets, all producing little fleas. Happily, there are a number of preparations on the market which provide effective and reasonably prolonged protection around the house.

TICKS

Another external parasite that you may come across, particularly if you live in the country or walk your dog where sheep have grazed, is the tick.

Ticks engorge on the blood of their host, and the engorged tick looks a little like a wart on the dog's skin and is occasionally mistaken for one by the dog's owner. Do not attempt to remove the tick by the traditional method of burning it off with a cigarette end – if it is a wart, it will be extremely painful for your dog – or by simply pulling it off. If pulled off, a tick leaves its mouth parts embedded in the dog's skin, and this, in time, will cause an abscess. To remove a tick safely, soak a piece of cotton wool in surgical spirit and hold it over the tick. As the tick dies, it releases its mouth and falls away intact.

COMMON AILMENTS

ANAL GLANDS
The anal glands are two scent glands situated on either side of the anus, which should empty every time faeces are passed, depositing their contents as a scent marker. If, for some reason, they fail to empty, they can become too full and cause irritation. If this is not relieved, the glands can soon become infected, and cause abscesses to form.

Symptoms of the anal glands impacting are your Bull Terrier dragging himself along on his bottom (known as 'playing daleks' in this family), a slight swelling in the anal area, or the

occasional whiff of a foul smell. Expressing these glands is a simple procedure, but best carried out by your veterinary surgeon, as inexperienced attempts could cause mild injury.

COUGHS

Coughing is a common symptom of many canine diseases. A harsh, dry cough could indicate kennel cough, and you should consult your vet for treatment. Kennel cough is highly contagious, and although it poses a relatively minor risk to adult dogs, it can prove to be fatal to very young puppies, old dogs, or dogs in poor health.

Coughing can also be caused by smoke or dust irritation, an infection such as bronchitis or laryngitis, distemper, or it may be a sign of heart disease. It could also be something as obvious as a foreign body lodged in your dog's throat. If the cough is persistent, or the dog is showing other symptoms, consult your vet immediately.

INTERDIGITAL CYSTS

Interdigital cysts are soft, painful swellings which form between the dog's toes. Usually the first indication is when you see your dog continually licking between his toes. The most effective treatment is a course of antibiotics prescribed by your friendly neighbourhood vet.

CUTS AND WOUNDS

There is bound to be a time during your Bull Terrier's life when he receives a cut or a wound. Treatment depends on the size and depth of the wound. If it looks deep, or longer than about one centimetre, it will probably require a stitch or two at the veterinary surgery. If you decide to take the dog to the vet, do nothing with the wound, unless it is bleeding profusely, as the nurse is likely to have to take longer cleaning your dressing off the wound than the stitching itself will take.

A minor cut, or a scratch that does not penetrate the skin, will usually need very little in the way of treatment. Soothing antiseptic cream will be sufficient for a scratch, and even that may do more to prolong healing than to help, by bringing the attention of the dog to the wound. Similarly, a small cut needs no particular attention, once you have trimmed the hair away, other than to keep the wound clean with a mild antiseptic solution, and to keep an eye open for any swelling, which could indicate infection.

HEAT EXHAUSTION

By far the commonest cause of heat exhaustion is when a dog is left in his owner's car in warm weather. The temperature inside a closed car in a British summer can kill a dog, and many have died in this way.

The signs of heat stress are obvious distress, heavy panting, and an inability to breathe deeply enough indicated by a half-strangled noise from the dog's throat. The dog's tongue looks swollen and blue.

Treat as an immediate emergency, and do not attempt to take the dog for veterinary treatment until you have started his resuscitation.

Plenty of cold water is the first-aid treatment. Ideally, immerse the whole dog in a bath (a cattle trough will do the trick if you are out on a walk). Bathe the dog all over with cold water, but especially its head. Keep doing it until the dog shows signs of easier breathing. Then, take your dog to the veterinary surgeon. The vet may put the dog on to an oxygen air flow, and will probably give him an injection to reduce the swelling in his throat. However, unless the vet happens to be nearby (for example, if you are at a dog show), the life-saving treatment will have been given before the dog gets to the surgery.

POISONING
Invariably, the poisons likely to be encountered by a Bull Terrier are those found around the house. They may include tablets

and medicaments intended for human consumption, or substances not for internal use at all, household chemicals such as bleach or detergents and garden chemicals.

Puppies will try anything. You must, therefore, keep all potentially dangerous substances out of their reach, and preferably in a locked cupboard.

If an accident should happen, and your dog appears to have eaten something that could be poisonous, give him an emetic immediately but only if it really can be immediately. If making the dog sick is to be of any help, it must be done before the poisonous substance has had a chance to be absorbed through the stomach. If your vet is immediately available for advice, and you are certain what it is the dog has eaten, do not make the dog sick until you have spoken. The most effective emetic is washing soda. Two small crystals are put on to the back of the dog's tongue, and the dog is made to swallow them by holding his mouth shut until he does. Vomiting will take place within minutes.

Retain as much of the substance, or at least its wrapping, as you can to take to the veterinary surgeon. Phone your vet and discuss the problem: he or she may be able to reassure you that there is likely to be no ill effect from the ingestion of the substance, or to recommend immediate further treatment.

STINGS

Most dogs, the Bull Terrier included, seem to be fascinated with bees and wasps and to derive great pleasure from trying to catch them. If the dog is successful, it is usually rewarded with a sting. If the sting is visible, remove it with a pair of tweezers, and apply a strong solution of bicarbonate of soda. Veterinary attention must be sought if the swelling is acute, or if the sting is in the dog's mouth or throat.

INHERITED CONDITIONS

KIDNEY DISEASE

The Bull Terrier is, in general, a hardy and healthy breed. However, prospective owners do need to be aware that some lines are affected by inherited kidney disease, and, as a consequence, you should make enquiries as to whether both parents of your puppy were examined for kidney disorders. Detection of hereditary kidney disease is usually a straightforward procedure, and is certainly advisable prior to using an animal for breeding.

Successful diagnosis and treatment of kidney disease can be problematic as there are often no discernible external symptoms during the early stages. However, an increased thirst is often as good a warning signal as any, and it is advisable to have a sample of your dog's urine tested. Early detection enables effective treatment which will prolong your dog's life.

HEART DISEASE
Another health problem affecting the Bull Terrier is heart disease. In some cases, this is no more than a slight murmur, and does not affect the dog's quality of life at all. Other cases may be more serious.

If you are considering breeding from your Bull Terrier, you must ensure that your dog is physically fit, and you should consider a heart test, carried out by your veterinary surgeon, as essential.

DEAFNESS
Inherited deafness is an occasional problem in Bull Terriers.

It can be detected from an early age, and schemes are now available in many countries to test puppies at about six weeks of age.

THE OLDER DOG
As a Bull Terrier enters old age, he will slow down and often find it difficult to do much of what was taken for granted when he was in his prime. It is highly likely that the dog will develop arthritis, and also that his hearing and eyesight may fail.

As time goes by, your Bull Terrier may require medication to help with an age-related condition. It is essential that you seek veterinary advice and follow instructions faithfully in order to provide your dog with a pain-free retirement.

With old age a Bull Terrier's meals, although reduced in quantity, should be increased in frequency – almost a return to a puppy feeding regime. This will decrease the strain put on internal organs by providing food little and often rather than in one or two larger meals.

Caring for the veteran Bull Terrier does require patience and

understanding, and perhaps even a few lifestyle changes. However, with a few minor adjustments, many Bull Terriers enjoy their twilight years, and so do their owners!

THE LAST GOODBYE

Although modern veterinary science has advanced a great deal and gone some way to reduce the effects of age-related ailments in dogs, it is sad to say that our four-legged friends still do not live nearly as long as we would like them to. The Bull Terrier, on average, lives for approximately ten years, although some make much older bones and others die regrettably young.

It is perhaps every dog owner's wish that their canine companion, when the time comes, dies peacefully in his sleep. However, if your Bull Terrier becomes old and infirm, his 'quality of life' should be uppermost in your mind.

Too many owners put off making the final decision, not out of concern for their dog, but to spare their own feelings.

Your Bull Terrier will have led an active and happy life, providing you and your family with loyalty and companionship. If he becomes incontinent or crippled with arthritis, your dog will lose his dignity and pride. When this happens, you, as the

The older dog deserves special consideration.

owner, have a duty to your dog to see that he leaves this world peacefully and with his dignity and pride intact, rather than prolonging a life that is becoming increasingly miserable.

Although your Bull Terrier's passing will leave a huge void in your life, time really does heal, and, gradually, you and your family will remember the fun and good times you all had together. Eventually, you will remember the delight you felt when you first saw that naughty little face. And that is when it all begins again!